ToP TiPs 2

A refreshing blend of brand new handy hints plus others hand picked from the pages of

ISBN 1 870870 67 0

Published in Great Britain
by John Brown Publishing Limited,
The Boathouse, Crabtree Lane,
Fulham, London SW6 6LU.

First printing October 1995.

Printed and bound in Great Britain by
BPC Paperbacks Ltd

Viz To

CONT

House & Home
A hotch potch of handy household hints . . . . *page 5*

Love & Sex
Trouser arousing tips for lovers young and old *17*

Cookery & Catering
A cuisine cacology for the kitchen *21*

Hobbies & Horticulture
Gelastic garbage for gardeners,
DIY enthusiasts, etc. *27*

Mend & Make Do
Eximious excersizes in thrift and economy *31*

Trains & Boats & Planes
Travelling tips and hints for holidaymakers *41*

Retail & Commercial
A penny pinching, shilly shallying
shopping list *45*

Driver & Vehicle
Motoring marvels for the dexterous driver *51*

ips 2

ENTS

Science & Technology
Impelling ideas and ingenious inventions 57

Eat, Drink & Be Merry
A feast of frivolity for winers and diners 61

Tinkers, Tailors, Soldiers & Sailors
Words of wisdom for weary workers 65

Mind & Body
A weird and witless route to health and fitness 71

Style & Panache
Dandy devices for fops and coxcombs 77

Veterinary & Zoological
Prudence for pets and animal lovers 81

Fun & Games
An encyclopedia of enjoyment and sporting
suggestions 87

Cheese & Onion
Anything that wouldn't fit into the previous
15 categories 93

Edited by Chris Donald

Written by Chris Donald, Graham Dury,
Simon Thorp, Simon Donald
and the many readers of Viz magazine
too numerous to be paid.

Illustrated in remotest Wales by Davey Jones.
Additional illustrations by Boco Perez after Jones.

A new selection of Top Tips appear in every issue of Viz.
Editorial address: Viz, P.O. Box 1PT,
Newcastle upon Tyne, NE99 1PT.

"**Darling** *I adore your new arrangement of the furniture. How do you manage it by yourself?*"

IT'S SO EASY—JUST PEEL OFF THE PROTECTIVE BACKING LIKE THIS

Chapter One

HOUSE & HOME

'A comfortable house is
a great source of happiness'.
Sydney Smith

KEEP old light bulbs after they 'pop'. When your neighbour asks you to look after his house while he's away on holiday, swap them for some of his.

> P. Legg
> Lyndhurst

SAVE on expensive loo roll by taking a gripping book to the toilet with you. You'll become so engrossed that whatever there was to wipe will have dried up by the time you put the book down.

> M. Armalade
> Teddington Lock

PSYCHICS. Take advantage of electric night storage heating. Simply predict the next day's weather correctly, 24 hours in advance, every single day, and hey presto! A perfectly heated house every morning.

> M. Barr
> Gloucester

SHAPE rusty iron filings into dog turds. When flies eat it they will be too heavy to take off and can be easily caught with a magnet.

> Paul Kelly
> Wimbledon

MAKE a miniature 'mouse trap' for flies by using a spring-loaded wooden clothes peg, baited with a winnit.

> T. Hawthorns
> West Bromwich

A GOOD book with all the pages covered in cellophane makes for ideal reading in the shower.

> S. Adam
> London

KEEP monkeys out of your kitchen by hiding bananas on top of a wardrobe in your bedroom.

> Mrs D.
> Includes-Underlay
> Andfitting

GIVE your house that 'city centre car park' feel by putting 'P' and 'NO SPACES' signs on the front door, and inviting tramps in to urinate down your stairs.

> D.U.
> Hong Kong

WHEN leaving your house empty, nip across into your neighbour's garden and prize open one of their windows. This will make their house a far more attractive proposition to burglars than your own.

> Mr G. Woodward
> Gillingham

OLD folks. Foil the VAT man this winter by clambering up on top of a bookcase, cupboard or wardrobe. Warm air rises, and so the temperature will increase the higher you climb.

B. Park
Oldham

MAKE the postman think you are sexually active by opening the door each morning looking tired, but grinning broadly.

Andrew Petrie
Kidderminster

AVOID sky high electricity bills, a dry stuffy house and stained walls by telling the electricity company to stuff their electric central heating up their arses.

T. Wicks
Fulham

SAVE the call charge next time you dial a wrong number by replacing your receiver before the phone is answered.

> Mike Way
> Frodingham

IMPROVE the quality of your junk mail by always ticking the 'over £60,000' income box on market research questionnaires.

> Mary Grinstead
> Forest Hill, London

CREATE the impression of bats in your attic by pinning used 'one cup' tea bags by their strings to the roof beams.

> K. Newton
> Burnley

PUT paid to the expression 'the grass is always greener on the other side of the fence' by having your lawn concreted over.

> B. Bounty
> Rochester

MAKE sure your neighbour hasn't wired his house up to your electricity supply by asking him to turn on every electric appliance in his house, then sit and watch your meter to see whether it is moving any faster.

> F.D.
> Cardiff

INCREASE blind people's electricity bills by switching all their lights on when their guide dog isn't looking.

> P.F.
> Stanley

ASK double glazing contractors to fill your new sealed window units with water and dessicated coconut. Rapidly opening and closing the windows will then create an instant 'snowstorm' effect.

> H. Head
> Wooler

GET rid of bats by attaching mouse traps to helium filled balloons and releasing them at night.

> B. Newton
> Liverpool

SMASH the entire contents of your home with a sledge hammer before going away on holiday. Then any would be burglars who break in will get a taste of their own medicine.

> Mrs Ena Brown
> Wolverhampton

AVOID getting Cornflakes or Muesli encrusted to your husband's clothes by keeping cereal packets and washing powder boxes in separate kitchen cupboards.

Mrs B. Murdoch
Bedford

KEEP your washing machine clean when out of use by leaving it running on the 'hot whites wash' setting.

T. Foster
Alton

SAFELY dispose of old neon lighting tubes by inserting them carefully into a dead snake.

M. Chivers
London

IN hot weather attach a length of string to a homing pigeon's leg and tie the other end to your ceiling rose. The bird will try to fly home, but instead will simply circle the room, creating a cooling breeze with its constantly flapping wings. Place bread crumbs and water on a step ladder in the middle of the room so that it can stop occasionally for a rest and some refreshment.

Mr N. Bus
Haymarket

IGNORE advice to leave a light on when you go out, in case of burglars. If anyone is heartless enough to break into your home, they should jolly well be left to find the light switches for themselves. Making things easier for them will only encourage these people to commit more crime.

H. Stevenage
Northumberland

ARMCHAIR football fans. Create a real stadium atmosphere in your sitting room by sharing your armchair with two or three fat neighbours. Get your wife to sit on the floor in front of you, and tell her to stand up whenever anything exciting happens.

> Pippa Legg
> Lyndhurst, Hants.

PENSIONERS. Avoid the embarrassment of having your swollen, badly beaten face shown on the front cover of newspapers by keeping a reasonable amount of cash in your home. Only if your attacker nets a paltry amount will the tabloids show any interest.

> A. Anderson
> Hereford

WEAR a miner's helmet in bed. Not only does it provide emergency light in the event of power failure, but it also protects against unexpected falls of plaster from the ceiling.

> Mr M. G. Midget
> Harwich

RECREATE the fun of a visit to a public swimming pool in your own home by filling the bath with cold water, adding two bottles of bleach, then urinating into it, before jumping in.

> Mrs S. Poole
> Bath

OLD FOLKS. Stay warm and safe this winter by wrapping yourselves in aluminium foil. Not only will this conserve vital body heat, but it will also make you look a bit like 'Robocop', thus going some way towards deterring would be burglars.

> S. Holmes
> York

A SIMPLE car theft prevention technique can be put to effective use on houses too. Have your house number engraved on your front window. Would-be thieves will then think twice before breaking in.

> J. Begley
> Timperley

SMOKERS. Take the effort out of stubbing out cigarettes by placing a used, damp tea bag at the bottom of your ashtray.

> Chris Douglass
> Stafford

CROOKLOCKS designed to secure car steering wheels can just as easily be fastened to a toilet seat, thus preventing burglars from using your lavatory.

> J.B.
> Timperley

FILL the bath with water, then add 14 kilos of salt. Hey presto! Your own miniature 'Dead Sea'.

> Steven James
> Stoke on Trent

CONVINCE visitors you are a cat lover by taking a razor blade to your furniture and urinating regularly behind your settee.

> B. Moore
> London E17

A DROP of cooking oil outside a mouse hole will help get rid of the rodents. When they next appear, they will slip over onto their backs, making capture much easier.

> Lynne Bordessa
> Allerton

KEEP all your CDs in the wrong cases. If a burglar steals them, at least he'll have the unenviable task of sorting them out before he can sell them to his 'fence'.

> P. Legg
> Lyndhurst

WHEEL clamps can probably be used to secure dust-bin lids to the ground, thus preventing them from being stolen, or blown away on windy nights.

> J.B.
> Timperley

ToP TiPs 2

PAINT slices of cork yellow and leave them on the floor. It's texture makes it almost indistinguishable from cheese, however mice will not touch it as they are unable to nibble cork.

> M. Haworth
> Crumpsall

IF you have a squeaking door, leave the house and walk fifty yards down the street. From this distance it is unlikely you will be able to hear it.

> Mr S. F. Chicken
> Walter Wilsons

POLO mints scattered around the floor will deter mice from entering the room. They have a strong aversion to peppermint.

> L. Haworth
> Crumpsall

GIVE passers-by the impression that you own a cat by littering your garden with decapitated sparrows and sawing a hole in the bottom of your back door.

> B. Moore
> London E17

SAVE the price of a new television licence by simply keeping your old one and only watching repeats which you've already paid for.

> S. Filler
> Fulchester

FIND out whether programmes you've watched on television were any good or not by reading Gary Bushell's column in The Sun.

> Alice Cydon
> Finsbury Park

IMPRESS the neighbours' children by climbing onto your roof and then walking a couple of yards off the edge. Don't look down. Just bend down slowly, and tentatively probe the lack of 'ground' beneath you. Then stand up again, give a feeble wave, then plummet to the round with a crash.

> R. Runner
> Arizona

SHOE segs make ideal 'fridge magnets' for use on wooden cupboards etc.

> D. B.
> Harwich

DON'T throw away that old pianola just because the music rolls are no longer available from record shops. I find that a roll of kitchen paper makes an ideal substitute, although the tune can be somewhat repetitive.

> Mrs E. McLane
> Longbenton

A ROLLER skate with the wheels removed, painted yellow, makes a handy 'foot clamp' for anyone standing in your garden without permission.

> Mrs M. Burn
> Catton

MAKE your own orthopaedic car seat cover by threading conkers onto a string vest.

> Mr G. Walton
> Gosforth

Chapter Two

LOVE & SEX

'Sex is not a "thing" on its own, but part of a deep human relationship planned by God'
Cliff Richard, 1968

MAKE your wife cry when you're having sex by phoning her up and telling her.

R.G.
Manchester

WHY waste a fortune on expensive telephone sex lines? Just dial any number and forget to add the '1' after the first zero. The woman on the BT tape has got a really sexy voice, and the call is free.

Pippa Legg
Lyndhurst

A TUB of margarine, sent via InterFlora, is the perfect romantic gift for a girl who likes making sandwiches.

M. B.
Wakefield

FELLAS. Missus driving you up the wall? Make two pin pricks in your neck, then kill her with a mallet and a sharp piece of wood. Instead of arresting you, the cops will congratulate you for killing a vampire.

D. J. Bowen
Cardiff

PROLONG your love-making by inventing excuses to get up and go downstairs every thirty seconds or so (left the gas on, put the cat out, etc.) This way your love-making can last all night long.

S. Grey
Mudfastlieghshire

FELLAS. A fun way to keep warm on cold winter nights is to fill your inflatable sex doll with hot water.

Pete Turner
Garston

FELLAS. Avoid not getting a shag every time you forget your wife's birthday. Simply give her 30 cards all at once, with "Not to be opened until (date and year)" written on the envelopes. After 30 years she'll probably be so old and ugly she won't be worth shagging anyway, so it won't matter if you forget.

H. Foster
Gloucester

FED up with oral sex? Stop your bird from giving you blow jobs by marrying her.

M.A.
Leeds

FELLAS. Make your birds tits look bigger by viewing them through a magnifying glass.

G. Knox
Walsall

SMOKING after sex is much easier if you use a metal funnel as a cigarette holder. Insert the cigarette inside the funnel so that the funnel acts as an ashtray whilst you lie on your back. To tip the ash simply nod your head a couple of times.

H. Higson
Lincoln

BORED with shagging your wife? Then have sex in the 'doggy' position, using her back as a handy 'table' on which to position your porny magazines. You'll be aroused by all the pictures of dirty women, and she'll be so turned on by your improved performance she won't notice you occasionally turning the pages over.

L. Daglish
Kettering

TAKE a tip from Frankenstein. Before you go out drinking, tape a small battery to your cock. The tiny electrical charge will be enough to keep it stimulated, and no matter how much you drink you'll be 'Ever Ready' for sex.

M. Shelley
Ipswich

You cannot eat HEALTHY LIFE BISCUITS and fail to masticate them. . . . They are health food in its best form . . . definitely helpful in constipation . . . milled from the entire wheat berry. . . . They are packed in attractive tins which keep th_ crisp ready-to-eat and ready condition. NO HOUSEHOLD BE WITHOUT A TIN. 1/- P

Chapter Three

COOKERY
&
CATERING

'A chef is not what he
eats, but what he cooks'
Kim Wilde, 1988

"WHAT A MARVEL-
LOUS FLAVOUR THIS
BREAD HAS! WHERE
DID YOU GET IT?"

"MARY MAKES
ALL OUR BREAD
FROM PREWETT'S
FLOUR. IT SUITS
US BETTER THAN
ORDINARY
BREAD."

AFTER dinner, save the expense of a coffee percolator by simply putting fresh coffee in a pot and adding hot water. Then ask guests to wear an old stocking over their head whilst drinking to stop any bits getting in their mouth. The denier of the stocking can be changed according to whether you are drinking espresso or coarse ground.

P. Cotton
Wells, Somerset

DON'T waste money on expensive Swiss cheese. Just buy cheddar, and poke holes in it with an old knitting needle.

G. Dent
Boscombe

FUN-sized Mars bars make ideal normal-sized Mars bars, for dwarfs.

T. Dell
Southampton

DON'T waste money on expensive cheddar cheese. Simply buy Swiss cheese and fill the holes with butter.

G. Dent
Boscombe

KING-sized Mars bars make ideal normal-sized Mars bars, for giants.

T. Dell
Southampton

TINNED sweetcorn fans. Save yourself the bother of wiping your arse by emptying the tin straight into the toilet.

T.O.
Sussex

MUMS. Save money when buying skimmed milk by buying full fat milk instead, then simply diluting it at home with water.

> Mr C. Day
> Milton Keynes

NORMAL-sized Mars bars make ideal king-sized Mars bars for dwarfs, as well as fun-sized ones for giants.

> T. Dell
> Southampton

AVOID the expense of buying cashew nuts by soaking ordinary salted peanuts in boiling water overnight. By the morning they will be suitably tasteless, and can easily be bent into the characteristic 'boomerang' shape by tying weights to either end and balancing the nut on the sharp edge of a ruler.

> John Tait
> Morpeth

SWEDES make ideal (if not slightly small) turnips for people who don't like turnips.

> Mr Vic Ground
> Stoke on Trent

VEGETARIANS coming to dinner? Simply give them real meat. As they're always going on about how TVP, soya and nut cutlets are "indistinguishable from real meat nowadays", they won't notice the difference.

> S. Simpson
> Edgeware

AVOID rice from sticking together by boiling each grain separately. Use four saucepans simultaneously to speed up the process.

> David Dinsdale
> Warley

STRING dipped in tomato sauce makes perfect re-usable spaghetti for kids who don't like spaghetti. My kids never touch the stuff, and don't realise I've been serving them up the same bowl of string for over a year now.

> Mr Salmon
> Broccoli-Bake
> Grimsby

REDUCE the risk of burns by making tea using cold water. Then heat the pot in the microwave.

William Doughty
Bangkok

SKIN a tomato by simply eating it. Hey presto! The next day you are left with just the skin in the toilet pan.

John Tait
Thropton

SURPRISE your teenage son by putting cigarettes instead of candles on his birthday cake. Everybody cheer as he lights his first one up.

Mrs E. Hawes
Kettlebury

AVOID dropped oven gloves from landing on the dirty floor by attaching them to the ceiling by a short length of elastic. Immediately you remove them from your hands the gloves will fly back to the ceiling.

Mrs B. Harper
Stoke

A DIGESTIVE biscuit topped with tomato ketchup and a slice of processed cheese makes a popular 'mini pizza' for kid's parties.

Mrs J. Crooks
Grantham

SET UP a Haagen Dazs ice cream franchise next door to your local Weight Watchers clinic. Give away freebies to slim people and watch the fat fuckers squirm.

D. R.
Croydon

LUMPS of cheese make perfect 'Lego' style building bricks for kids. They're cheap and they're fun, and there's no trips to casualty every time they happen to swallow a piece. And they give a whole new meaning to the the idea of 'playing with your food'.

S. Filler
Fulchester

MUMS. Stop children putting their elbows on the table at meal times by covering the table top in cement, and sprinkling it with broken glass. Leave small circles clear for plates, cups etc.

R.C.
Ashington

METAL washers make delicious 'Polo' mints for sweet toothed robots.

Miss J. Fisher
South Shields

Chapter Four

HOBBIES
&
HORTICULTURE

'The opposite to doing something
is doing nothing'

Jimmy Hill, 1978

GARDENERS. Wrap seedling potatoes in a wire mesh before planting. Hey, presto! Ready cut chips at harvest time.

Basil Pigsfanny
Nottingham

BEE keepers. Keep bee hives in strawberry fields to get jam instead of honey.

D. Unwin
Highgate

HITCHCOCK fans. Offer to make your wife a sandwich, then drill a hole in the bedroom wall and watch her getting into the shower.

P. Todrie
Aberdeen

A HERD of cattle make a common sense replacement for noisy lawn mowers. Since buying mine I no longer need to mow the lawn, and never have to worry about the milkman being late.

Mrs R. Dunning
Leeds

LADIES. Cycling helmet too big? Place a panty liner beneath the rim for a snug fit. (But don't use the ones with wings or you'll look like Deputy Dawg).

Janet Forrest
Kendal

HITCHCOCK fans. Glue breadcrumbs to a climbing frame in your garden, then sit on a bench with your back to it. Once the frame is covered in birds, try making a run for the house.

P. Todrie
Aberdeen

GARDENERS. Impatient waiting for your new trees to grow? Why not simply buy small trees in a pot, and place them on top of telegraph poles?

M. Kinghorn
Sudbury

MAKE the bin man think your dustbin is a dead dalek by placing it upside down and filling it with water and Alka-Seltzer tablets. Then stand behind your back yard door, with crocodile clips attached to your testicles, saying "exterminate' and "out of control" over and over again.

E. S. Batey
Walsall

PILE litter neatly around your garden during the autumn. The bright colours are virtually indistinguishable from flowers during the winter months, especially if viewed whilst squinting, or from a great distance.

Mrs G. Richardson
Oxford

PREVENT getting lost on forest walks by scattering a trail of breadcrumbs behind you. When you decide to go home simply follow the trail all the way back.

H & G
Bavaria

IMPRESS friends with your knowledge of country ways when out walking by stopping suddenly, sniffing loudly once or twice, then hissing "Fox. Can you smell it?" under your breath. Repeat with badger, deer etc.

Andrew Wedderburn
Windermere

SCUBA divers. A deflated wheel barrow inner tube worn around the neck makes a stylish polo neck for your wet suit.

C. Boulton
Derby

WHEN on those forest walks scatter pebbles along the way in order to find your way back. The birds can't eat them, and you won't end up at some stupid witch's toffee house in the middle of nowhere.

H & G
Bavaria

THROW large, peeled carrots into your garden pond. They are indistinguishable from expensive Koi carp.

F.W. Adey
Wolverhampton

OPEN air swimming pools get little use in winter. So why not fill them with soil and grow flowers in them until the summer comes round again.

Glen Dale
Northumberland

Protecting hinges against rain.—G. Pain (Ashford).

Apron Addition

APRONS are now obtainable with a piece of gay towelling sewn on the front. The towelling is often dirty before the apron, but by fixing it on with press fasteners, a quick change is possible.—J. BAILEY (Manchester, 18).

Press studs

Towelling

Do Your Shoes Need Repairing?

How to Do Your Own Snobbing at Home By F. E PECKHAM

Torch fitted to shovel simplifies fetching coal in the dark. — A. W. (Essex).

Chapter Five

MEND
&
MAKE DO

'I have never owned a dustbin.
There is no such thing as rubbish'
Sir Winston Churchill, 1961

Why Purchase a New Gate When it is Quite a Simple Task to Renew the Old One?
By C. FRANKLIN

Four 2" nails

18"

5"

Device for removing Wellington boots.— E. Bowen (Pontnewydd).

RENEW the bottom of an old bucket by placing it on the kitchen table and drawing a line around the base. Cut out the circle and press it hard into the bottom of the bucket.

> Mike Howarth
> Manchester

THE wire top off a Champagne bottle makes a handy walking frame for lame mice.

> Graham Townend
> Shipley

COVER up circular holes in your kitchen table top by placing a round bread board over the top of them.

> Mike Howarth
> Manchester

A TREBOR soft mint and child's paint brush make an ideal curling stone and brush for gerbil 'Highland Games'.

> A.E.G.
> Liverpool

LAST year's 'Mutant Ninja Turtle' figures, painted red or blue, make ideal 'Power Rangers'.

> A.G.
> Liverpool

FILL a shoebox with snow, then shit on it. Hey presto! Expensive Belgian chocolates.

> Phil Thunderchunk
> Ipswich

POLO mints make ideal 'life belts' for earwigs. Except they they don't float. And they dissolve in water.

> A. E. Greenall
> Liverpool

A DROP of whisky rubbed regularly into woodworm infected furniture will make the woodworms too drunk to have sex, and therefore unable to reproduce.

> N.M.
> Anfield Plain

BY jogging to work behind the bus I am able to save 96p a day in bus fares.

> N. Holland
> Fareham

A CONDOM makes an ideal 'bin bag' for your pet hamster.

> Chris Poulton
> Knutsford

BY jogging to a restaurant behind a taxi my wife and I were able to save £5.80 in taxi fares last Saturday night.

> N. Holland
> Fareham

STOP to pick up the bodies of any small animals (rabbits, mice, weasels, etc) which you run over on the road, and keep them in the boot of your car. Once the boot is full you should have enough to make a fur coat - an ideal surprise gift for your wife.

> P. Parker
> Preston

DON'T buy Fairy Liquid. With the money you save from one bottle you'll be able to afford a meal in a restaurant, and someone else will do the dishes for you.

> B. Jones
> Biddlecombe

USE only economy packs of toilet roll, instead of expensive 'luxury' tissue. You'll find that invariably your fingers go through both. But the money you save buying cheaper paper can then be spent on a bar of soap to clean them with.

Mrs E. Sharp
Grunty Fen

AN empty sardine tin makes an ideal miniature five-a-side pitch for teams of ladybird footballers. A grain of sugar, rounded at the corners with a nail file, makes a useful ball. But be sure to coat it with bleach or weed killer. Otherwise the ladybirds will eat it.

A. E. Greenall
Liverpool 11

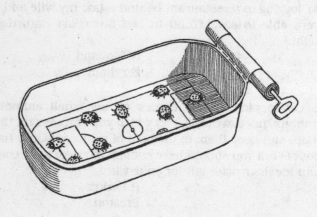

BY jogging to church behind a Rolls Royce carrying my daughter on my back I was able to save £125 in car hire charges at her recent wedding.

N. Holland
Fareham

PLASTIC tops from Smartie tubes make ideal frisbees for a pet gerbil, or hamster.

> Eric Waspbottom
> Nottingham

SAVE energy by placing solar powered calculators under a hat when not in use.

> Don Croy
> Surrey

USED lamp bulbs painted green make ideal 'pears', for display in a fruit bowl. They never rot, and will not attract insects.

> F. Cooper
> Ipswich

POP TARTS make ideal radiators for dolls' houses.

> N. Stiles
> Stockport

MALTESERS make ideal packing material for fragile objects being sent through the post. And the recipient can of course eat them without putting on weight.

> P.B.
> Chelsea

FARMERS. Don't throw away those old pairs of rubber kitchen gloves. With the ends of the fingers cut off they make ideal sexy 'peep hole' bras for cows.

> K. Newton
> Burnley

DON'T waste that left over carton of boiled rice. Colour the grains with felt tip pens to make slightly large and possibly toxic 'hundreds and thousands'.

> Mr Beech
> Braintree

MARBLES make ideal packing material for soft objects, such as pillows, being sent through the post.

P.B.

Chelsea

MAKE 'quiet' dice by compressing marshmallows into a cube shape, toasting them gently, and then painting dots on the side. Hey presto! The ideal gift for a deaf friend.

G. Banks

Stoke

SMALL lengths of rubber pipe make ideal 'skin tight body suits' for worms. Roll the worm in talcum powder first to ensure a comfortable fit.

K. Newton

Burnley

POSTAGE stamps make ideal temporary repairs for punctured tyres or inner tubes.

Mr M. Haworth

Crumpsall

BEER bottle tops floated upside down in the bath, make ideal 'dinghies' for spiders. Flies can also use them as aircraft carriers.

M. Harwood
Yeadon

THE TOP from a 'Bic' ballpoint pen makes an ideal Norman helmet for a worm.

John Tait
Thropton

THE LID from a sardine tin, with the key removed, makes an ideal quiff for a small robot.

I. Ink
Bootle

KEEP old Lottery tickets until Christmas. Cut into strips they make 'instant' paper chains for decorating your room with, and a useful reminder of how much money you've blown throughout the year.

Steven Wood
Nottingham

MAKE your own 'glitter' this Christmas by wrapping grains of sugar in kitchen foil.

> Mr T. Tunnel
> Jarrow

DURING cold weather a block of lard makes an inexpensive substitute for the more fangled modelling clays popular with children nowadays. And instead of being trodden into the carpet after use, it can be collected up and used to fry black pudding, etc.

> K. McGrath
> Duns

MAKE your own matches by painting a pea red, soaking it in petrol overnight, then pronging it on the end of a cocktail stick.

> G. Dawson
> Bletchley

OLD shoelaces should never be thrown away. Soak them overnight in petrol, roll them in lard, then pop them in the fridge for a few hours. Hey presto. Perfect candles.

> Rose Gray
> Godalming

MAKE your own extra large matches by soaking a glacier cherry in petrol then sticking it on the end of a wooden lollipop stick.

> G. Dawson
> Bletchley

'NIPPERS' from hermit crabs make ideal clothes pegs for Barbie dolls.

> John Tait
> Thropton

WELL chewed bubble gum makes an ideal sealant for around baths, sinks and work tops, and works out only eight times the cost of conventional silicon based sealants. Occasionally pick it off and chew it during idle moments in order to prevent it from drying out.

D. Holst
Beckenham

MAKE a giant 'high tar' cigarette by rolling up bark chippings in a roll of roofing felt, and not adding a filter.

G. Dawson
Bletchley

A RED balloon, full of petrol, tied to the end of a broom shank would make a perfect fairy tale giant's match.

G. Dawson
Bletchley

DISGUISE unsightly power station cooling towers as elephants feet by simply painting toenails on the bottom, and putting a giant 600 foot umbrella in the top.

Brian Johnson
Brighton

GIANT cigarettes can be made cheaply and easily using surplus household items. Simply roll up lawn clippings in a roll of old wallpaper, then pop an unused toilet roll in the end as a filter. You can light it using a giant match.

> G. Dawson
> Bletchley

BLIND people. Avoid getting dog shit on the end of your white stick by rolling a condom over the end. After a walk unroll the dirty condom and throw it in the bin.

> Gary 'Carpet'
> Axminster
> Bristol

CONVERT potatoes into convincing hand grenades by covering them in shoe segs, and painting them green.

> D.B.
> Harwich

A BANANA skin makes an ideal sun hat for a star fish.

> G. Hurst
> New Cross

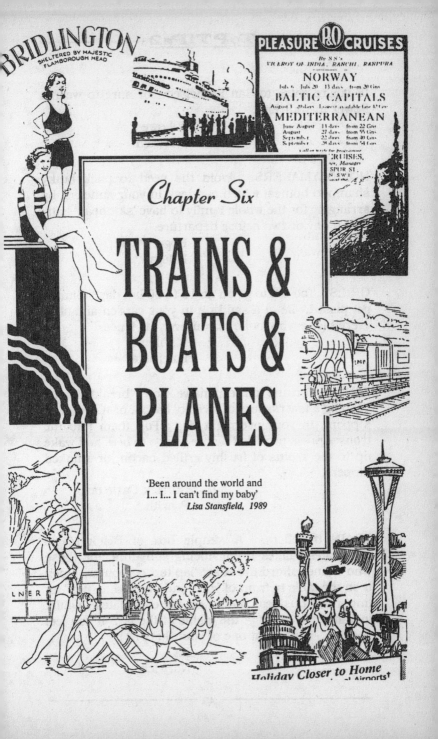

Chapter Six

TRAINS &
BOATS &
PLANES

'Been around the world and
I... I... I can't find my baby'
Lisa Stansfield, 1989

IF you're going to San Francisco, be sure to wear a flower in your hair.

P. Lowe
Norwich

HOLIDAYMAKERS. Avoid the need to pack bulky shampoo bottles, which can leak in your suitcase, by arranging for the whole family to have 'skinhead' hair-cuts a day or two before departure.

Roger Plynth
Polegate

GIRLS? Too old to go on an 18 to 30 holiday? Simply get pissed, lie in a sand pit in your garden and shag every bloke who looks at you over the fence.

S. Filler
Fulchester

SAVE a fortune on expensive hotel breakfasts by keeping a few rashers of streaky bacon, or a couple of kippers, in your overnight bag. Pop them into the trouser press provided before you go to bed, and wake up to the aroma of freshly grilled bacon, or smoked kippers.

Derrick Carleton
Penrith

TRAIN travellers. A simple box of Black Magic chocolates makes a convincing substitute for those who cannot afford the latest 'lap top' computer. Open it on the table in front of you, and pretend to 'type' an important business memo on the chocolates, whilst looking studiously at the inside of the lid. If you feel peckish, simply eat one of your 'keys'.

B.O.
Norwich

WHEN being photographed for a bus pass or railcard, wear a large hat, sun glasses and a big false moustache. The card can then be lent for use by any of your friends, along with the hat, sunglasses and false moustache.

John Harkness
Kesslemere

CONVINCE fellow train travellers that you're an off duty soldier by standing in the corridor at the end of the train drinking cans of beer. Add to the effect by occasionally falling out of the door to your death whilst the train is in motion.

Mrs Anne Field
Kirby

HOLIDAY makers. Prevent postmen from reading your post cards by sending them all in a sealed envelope to one trusted friend, together with a note asking your friend to deliver them all by hand.

Lorraine Quiche
Banbury

PLANE passengers. Always volunteer to sit next to that portly passenger who is having difficulty fitting into his or her seat. If the plane crashes in snow covered mountains you can survive for months by eating the blubbery bastard.

G. Hose
Shed

COACH passengers. When travelling abroad always pack your passport near the top of your suitcase, and ask the driver to leave your suitcase handy near the front of the boot. This greatly reduces the time spent rummaging around for it at border crossings etc.

K. Dee
Monaco

TRAVEL free on trains by looking like a bicycle and leaning against a wall in the corridor.

> Scott Shaw
> Hemel Hempstead

STOP German holiday makers hogging all the deck chairs this summer by getting them to sign an agreement promising not to. Then return to your hotel room and wave it in the air, saying "I have in my hand a piece of paper".

> Phil Bert
> Leicester

PLANNING holidays is half the fun. So why not stay at home this year and plan two? Just as much fun, and it costs absolutely nothing.

> R. Rolaston
> Redhill

HUNDREDS OF PRICE CUTS!

EASY TERMS YOU CAN AFFORD

SAFEWAY Double Concentrated TOMATO PUREE

Buy BRITISH Buy BEST

Plus FREE TROUSERS

£14.99 Sale Price
£29.99 Sale Price
£29.99 Sale Price
£79.99 Dixons Deal

Buy Now Pay July '96 —OR— 10 MONTHS INTEREST FREE

OFFER PRICE £1.00* FIRST 5 CUSTOMERS FRI, SAT & SUN

CREAMED RICE PUDDING DEVON CREAM

Chapter Seven

RETAIL & COMMERCIAL

10% EXTRA DISCOUNT FOR SENIOR CITIZENS

Fresh Milk Semi-Skimmed

'Shopping patterns are changing. By the year 2000 there will only one shop left. And it will be on the Moon'
Sir John Hall, 1989

GET THERE FAST WHILE STOCKS LAST!

We want you to say YES Motel Strip

U.S. 101 – Near Golden Gate Bridge

MOTELS · RESTAURANTS · GAS STATION

Fair Trades APPROVED

CONFUSE shopkeepers by buying a sheet of wrapping paper and asking them to wrap it.

D. Treloar
Wandsworth

WHEN applying for a mortgage from the Midland Bank claim to be Brazilian. That way, if you fail to keep up the re-payments, the bank will simply write off your debt.

Jesus Pele Carambos
Cricklewood

WHEN shopping for a ruler or tape measure always measure the one you intend to buy with another one before paying for it, thus ensuring that the measurements on the one you are buying are accurate.

Mr C. Bourbon
Hereford

SUPERMARKET cashiers. Why not simply have love bites tattooed on your necks. That way there would never be any danger of you being without one.

E. Banger
Walsall

GREENGROCERS Why throw away old, shrivelled, unsold fruit and veg? Simply label it 'Organic Produce' and charge twice the usual price.

P.T.
Liverpool L19

ELECTRICAL retailers. Deter ram raiders by putting mirrors in your windows, causing criminals to swerve at the sight of their own car, thus hitting the shop next door.

R. Jar
Tottenham

FELLAS. When out shopping, be careful not to get Bin Liners and Pantie Liners confused. I have it on good authority that neither is much good as a substitute for the other.

Tony Silver
Newbury

SHOPKEEPERS. If the electrical retailer next door puts mirrors in his window, check your insurance cover in case a car swerves and crashes into your shop.

R. Jar
Tottenham

FURTHER depress the owners of unprofitable and rapidly failing tacky seaside gift shops by crossing the road purposefully in their direction, before veering off at the last moment.

Anon.
Shanklin, I.O.W.

RAM raiders. Make sure you use someone else's car when smashing into shop fronts. On a recent raid I netted goods worth over £1000. But the damage to my car came to £2,700.

A. Smith
Gateshead

TEENAGERS. If a shopkeeper refuses to sell you cigarettes because you don't look old enough, take him to the nearest bus stop. When a bus comes ask the driver for a child's fare. When he says you don't look young enough, leave the pair of them to argue about it, while you go back to the shop and steal the fucking cigarettes.

Russel Whyte
Dundee

KEEP Sunday Special campaigners. Wear a large yellow hat at all times. Shopkeepers can then put up signs saying 'Sorry - we do not serve people with yellow hats on Sundays'. That way everyone will be happy.

> G. Widdle
> Swansea

WHEN buying fruit by the pound, buy grapes instead of apples. Apples are much heavier.

> Edna Thompson
> Bishopsgate

FAIRY Liquid bosses. Dilute your washing up liquid with water. Then you won't need to spend so much money on TV adverts telling people how strong it is.

> Y. Bell
> Norfolk

CIGARETTES are a much cheaper and more widely available alternative to nicotine patches.

> B. Carr
> Nottingham

SHOPPERS. Take the leg work out of shopping by simply standing at the supermarket check-out and removing any items you require from other people's trolleys as they approach.

> S. O'Keefe
> Waterford

WHEN buying a computer make sure you get 'state of the art' equipment by asking the man who delivers it to take it back and change it for the new model that has invariably superceded it during the two weeks in which you were waiting for it to arrive.

> R. Daltrey
> Gosforth

TAKE £100 with you every time you visit a cashpoint. If the machine refuses to give you any money, avoid embarrassment by pretending to remove this wad from the machine, then walk away smiling.

> Waz
> Liverpool

INSIST on showing the chemist all your holiday snaps when you go to pick them up after having them developed. It must be frustrating for them never getting to see anyone's snaps. If there are people queuing behind you, show the pictures to them next so they don't feel left out.

> J. Howey
> Oswestry

DON'T write your PIN number on the back of your cash card because you won't be able to read it once you've put it in the machine.

> William Quibble
> Fyfield

STUDENTS. When visiting the cinema ensure that a long queue has formed behind you and that the cashier has already issued a full price ticket before you ask for a student discount.

> A cinema manager
> Berkshire

P.S. Oh, and while you're at it, don't forget to pay with a fucking credit card.

CREATE your own cash dispenser by lying your toaster on its side. Put £50 in ironed banknotes in one slot, then enter your bank card in the other. Then set the toaster. After a short while 'pop!' Out comes your cash, together with your returned card. (Always use a low setting to prevent your money from catching fire or your card from melting.)

> K. Carr
> London SW1

DON'T waste money on gift vouchers this Christmas. Try giving bank notes. These are available in a variety of sizes, colours and denominations, and are accepted by most High Street shops.

> C. McKeown
> Fleetwood

VICARS. Drum up more business this winter by dressing as Santa Claus and starting your Christmas services in early October.

> D. Robinson
> Cramlington

Chapter Eight

DRIVER & VEHICLE

'Papa'
Nicole, 1993

CAR commuters. Experience the thrills and spills of running to catch a bus by dashing from your car into the house after work only to see your wife slowly carrying the TV set away into the next room.

C. Paper
Tunbury

WHEN approaching a green light slow down and stop, in case Billy Idol is coming the other way on a motorbike.

W. Kirkpatrick
Toxteth

IF your brakes fail whilst driving at speed release your bonnet catch. The raised bonnet will provide vital wind resistance and help slow down the vehicle.

V. Ground
Hartlepool

MOTORWAY drivers. Ring up John Major's innovative 'Cones Hotline' and order a Flake '99' with raspberry sauce and hundreds and thousands on it.

N. McArthur
Uxbridge

IF your brakes fail whilst reversing, open all your car doors, and if possible the boot. Similarly, these will greatly increase wind resistance and help bring the vehicle to a standstill.

V. Ground
Hartlepool

RACE track owners . 'Sleeping policemen' and other traffic calming measures would help reduce the number of serious accidents during Grand Prix races.

Mrs S. F. Brains
Winchester

TAKE the trauma out of serious road traffic accidents by replacing your driver's air bag with a large Whoopee cushion. You'll still be laughing even while you're being cut from the wreckage.

Rob Hill
Wolverhampton

WHILE out driving try using this catchy rhyme to help remember what the different traffic lights mean. I find it most useful as I approach busy junctions.

When the red light does shine,
we must stop at the line.
When the amber is there,
we should all take good care.
But when the green light does show,
then off we may go.

Mrs P. Madeley
Rawdon

SALES reps. Place an 'honesty box' on the dashboard of your car. Every time you speed, fine yourself £5. At the end of each year the money you raise can then be used to buy a large fully equipped hospital to treat all the people who've been killed or injured as a result of your wreckless driving.

B. B.
Newmarket

HOLIDAYMAKERS. When catching a ferry or Euroshuttle train, jack your car's wheels up off the ground, put your car in gear and continue to 'drive' at exactly the same speed the boat or train is travelling. This will ensure your mileometer shows the true distance your car has travelled during your entire journey.

A. Nugget
Northumberland

BUS drivers. Before complaining about them not having the right change, ask the passenger who has just boarded your bus if he or she would mind walking to the back window to see whether or not it is clear for you to pull out again from the bus stop. If it isn't you can then pull out anyway, causing cars to brake sharply, whilst at the same time sending the passenger sprawling as they attempt to make their way back down the bus.

R. Kerr
Sunderland

STUCK for plates on your picnic? Simply remove your car wheel trims. Voila! Ideal for sausage rolls and chicken breasts.

Ma Wazzer
Liverpool

HGV drivers. When driving up hills the 'crawler' lane is the one on the fucking *left*.

Mr. F.R.T.
Cardiff

ALWAYS carry a tin of white paint and a paint brush in the boot of your car. If your chosen car park is full, simply paint an additional parking space for yourself.

Margaret B. Dickinson
Burnley

KNIGHT RIDER fans. Paint your Ford Sierra black and attach red fairy lights to the bonnet. Then drive to a gay bar and ask a particularly camp bloke to record a few words onto a cassette for you. Play it back as you're driving along, and hey presto! All the girls will mistake you for that lanky arsehole off 'Baywatch'.

Hec & Ham
Milton Abbey, Dorset

REMAIN on your toes when driving by cutting out a picture of a police car and glueing it onto your rear view mirror.

> Mr C. Savoury
> Yeovil

ALWAYS flash your hazard warning lights, or stick a raised thumb out of the window, after forcing your way into a flow of fast moving traffic. This friendly gesture will ensure that the driver behind you quickly forgets the emergency stop you caused him to make, and will more than make up for any rear end collision damage he has suffered from the car behind.

> David Connor
> Chingford

MAKE yourself drive more carefully in built up areas by cutting out pictures of children playing football and glueing them to the sides of your windscreen.

> Mr C. Savoury
> Yeovil

MAKE it look like your car smokes by sticking a roll of white paper in the exhaust pipe. Simple.

> Stephen Dunn
> Lilishaw

TIN foil custard tart dishes glued to your front bumper make cheap and economical replacements for expensive fog lamps.

> L. Hall
> Morpeth

LEAVE your sidelights on all day to make distant oncoming drivers think you might be driving a Volvo.

> P. Delaney
> Greenhills, Dublin

DON'T sell that old banger for scrap! Simply paint it white, with a big orange stripe down the side, and stick an old Cornflakes packet on the roof with 'POLICE' painted on it. Hey presto! The perfect deterrent for burglars.

> Ken Illingworth
> Luton

VOLVO drivers. Confuse distant oncoming drivers by removing the bulbs from your sidelights.

> P. Delaney
> Greenhills, Dublin

ALWAYS put 'pay and display' parking tickets upside down and in the centre of your windscreen in the hope that the parking warden will crick his neck trying to read it.

> S. Lyall
> Dundee

HEARSE drivers. Try attaching flashing yellow lights to your roof, the way that other slow moving vehicles do. I don't wish to appear disrespectful, but I'm sure grieving relatives would find a few flashing lights a lot more dignified than a car skidding into the back of the deceased, sending the coffin flying out through the front windscreen.

> A. Rayleigh
> Sidcup

LORRY drivers. Look down the wrong end of a pair of binoculars when driving on the motorway. This will enable you to drive even closer to the back of my fucking car.

> L. Ripper
> Westward Ho!

Chapter Nine

SCIENCE
&
TECHNOLOGY

'Elec-trical banana is going
to be the very next thing'
Donovan, 1967

Ex-ter-min-ate! A

"It's the Goods!"

The vaporizer is
the best thing I
ever saw and I
have seen many
good things

The Hyo-Glossus
(Singing Muscle)

AVOID 'red eye' when taking flash photographs by sticking a small piece of black tape over the flash bulb on the front of your camera.

> D. Burton
> Felling

SATELLITE TV enthusiasts. Save the expense of a motorised dish system by installing a fixed dish to the roof of your car. Then simply drive round in small circles until you locate the satellite of your choice.

> John Kean
> M.D.
> Satcom Europe Ltd.

NOW that an increasing number of products are no longer tested on animals it makes sense to keep several household pets in order that you can carry out your own tests, as and when required.

> Iris Pissier
> Hull

EAT whilst watching TV without having to take your eyes off the screen for a second. Simply cover your plate with tin foil and wire it up to your fork with a battery and bell. If the fork touches an area of plate with no food on it, the bell will sound and you can simply try again.

> Dave Simpson
> Tring

REPAIR broken light bulbs by replacing the old glass with a partly inflated white balloon. Put it in the freezer to make it go hard.

> K. Black
> Alnwick

PLACE your television in the porch and sit outside watching movies through the letter box. Hey presto! An instant 'wide screen' effect at no extra cost.

> D. Scott
> Buxton

MUMS. Fit an extra handle onto your pram so that it can be pushed either way.

> Mike Howarth
> Manchester

ADULT CHANNEL bosses. Add at least five million names to your subscription list by scrambling your signal before the 'Dish of the Day' gets her kit off.

> J. Kean
> London SE1

GET extra shine from your light bulbs without even changing them. Simply rewire them with thicker flex, thus allowing much more electricity into the bulb.

> K.Black
> Alnwick

EAT soup whilst watching TV by wiring up a simple lighting circuit, with two terminals in your bowl. When both are exposed to air and the plate is empty, the circuit brakes and a light above the TV will go off. Wear rubber gloves for extra safety whilst eating.

> Dave Simpson
> Tring

CUT electricity bills in half by changing the flex on all your electrical appliances for a much thinner one which will only allow half of the electricity through.

> K. Black
> Alnwick

TOASTERS make ideal 'daredevil' cannons for flat fish such as flounder, sole or turbot. But fish should be careful to perform this trick on dry land only, as water is an excellent conductor of electricity.

> Sean Phillips
> Monifieth, Dundee

ATTACH a 'bayonet' to your TV remote control by taping a fork to it. This way you can keep control of the television whilst eating TV snacks.

> A. Cowie
> Duns

POTATOES make interesting if not entirely functional replacements for light bulbs.

> Mrs B.Durks
> Essex

Colman's Mustard

THE MUSTARDEERS' OATH

We will have Mustard whenever we can get it. Mustard makes good food taste better.

We **will** have Mustard—

Learn to EAT!

Learn which foods pe... ...em—which ...as medicines. Find ou... ...foods sho...
...ever be combined at t... ...Learn whi...
...oods help Arthritis, ...ation —
...whatever your particular ... ...ow knowled...
...f Scientific Nutrition... ...bringing n...
...found health and happ... ...who had tri...
...everything else without... ...you, too, c...
...learn these vital se... ...of your hon...
...lf you are sti... ...wes it to yo...
...self and ... ...this mode...
...road to

Chapter Ten

EAT, DRINK & BE MERRY

'Eat, drink and be merry.
For tomorrow we die'
Luke (Goss), 1988

You're so right with a Kaymet

PRETEND your house is a pub by stubbing out cigarettes on the carpet, watering your cans of beer and kicking your wife out into the garden at 11.30.

> Dave Upton
> Hereford

FLATULENT people. When you go out always keep a 'Whoopee cushion' in your back pocket. As you're about to fart, simply sit down, then produce the cushion from behind you whilst laughing childishly.

> C. Ground
> Nottingham

TAKE a selection of your old vinyl records along with you next time you go to an overpriced pizza restaurant. Take examples of a '45' single, an old '78' and a '33' long playing album, and use them to demonstrate to the idiot waiter exactly what size pizza you require. When it arrives, check it against your record to make sure it's the right size.

> M. Hepworth
> Halifax

FELLAS. Avoid pissing on the lavatory floor during the night after an evening of heavy drinking by nailing a pair of slippers to the floor directly in front of the toilet. Later, when you roll out of bed and stagger into the bathroom, simply slide your feet into the slippers and voila! You're in the perfect position for a piss.

Mr I. Stadium
Gateshead

P.S. For bowking assume a kneeling position with your knees in the slippers.

SMOKERS. Save £££s every year on matches and cigarette lighters by simply lighting your cigarette with the butt of your previous one.

T. O'Meara
Brighton

SAVE the expense of buying a plastic 'red nose' on Comic Relief day by simply drinking heavily for years on end until your own nose becomes red and swollen.

I. P. Head
Middlesbrough

GIRLS in the pub. Don't sing or hum along with the jukebox. You sound shit and embarrass your boyfriend.

A. Smith
Fulchester

TRAMPS. Stand with a paper cup next to the nearest bottle bank. Ask everyone to pour any remaining drops from their bottles into your cup. Within a few minutes you will have a free cup full of alcoholic punch.

Mr T. Tart
Sainsburys

A GLASS full of Marmite, topped with shaving foam, makes a quite convincing pint of Guinness, and has the advantage of tasting nicer.

Barry Carlisle
Froam

LADIES. When invited out to dinner in a fashionable restaurant always bring a fire blanket with you in your bag. Nowadays it is the foolhardy fashion for waiters to set fire to the pudding, and there is always a risk that the blaze could get out of control.

Miss B.Baxter
Potters Bar

NIGHTCLUB owners. Cut out trouble in one fell swoop by simply banning professional footballers.

G. Lane
Bury

POPPING two 'Alka Seltzer' tablets into a newly opened can of beer has exactly the same effect as a 'widget', and has the added advantage of preventing hang overs.

C. Atkinson
Windsor

Chapter Eleven

TINKERS, TAILORS, SOLDIERS & SAILORS

'Take all the work you can, because there will
be many years when no-one will want you'
Harold Davison (Tony Blackburn's manager), 1967

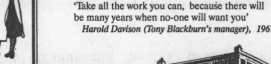

VICARS. Avoid confetti problems in your churchyard by spraying the bride and groom with a light coating of 'spray mount' adhesive before they leave the church. The confetti will then stick to them, and not be left littering the ground.

> John Kean
> New Malden

DENTISTS. Why pay over the odds for a fancy hydraulic chair? Simply strap patients to an ordinary wooden chair suspended from the ceiling on elastic rope. Lower or raise the patient to the required position by skilfully positioning weights in their various pockets.

> J. K.
> New Malden

JOHN MAJOR. Avoid having to pay subsidies to opera and sport by introducing a new tax on the poor, the stupid and the hopelessly optimistic. Call it the National Lottery.

> A. Anderson
> Aston

MURDERERS. Avoid 'capital' punishment by committing your crimes in provincial cities such as Manchester.

> F. Grunblatt
> Sunderland

GUN clubs. Ban quiet, shy men who tend to 'keep themselves to themselves'. Invariably these are the people who go berserk and carry out random, pointless shootings of innocent passers by.

> T. Starlet
> Arbroath

FARMERS. Rid your land of 'New Age Travellers' by burning down the village Post Office. If they can't cash their giros, they'll soon move on.

S. Hanna
Liverpool

ILLEGAL immigrants. Convince people that you're Scottish by drinking whisky, wearing women's clothes and a ginger wig, and throwing big logs around your back garden.

Jock McPatel
Stenhousemuir

CITY gents. Simulate the thrills of ski jumping by leaning forward and placing your umbrella under your arm next time you go down an escalator.

Matty
Liverpool

BLUES Brothers. Take your hats off and hey presto!
Reservoir Dogs.

> Damien Jeffrey
> London

PEOPLE whose surname is Toblerone should always
take along an empty 'Toblerone' chocolate box when
attending interviews for office jobs. This would save
your potential employer the expense of having to make
a name triangle for your desk, and therefore increase
your chances of getting the job.

> Mike Haworth
> Crumpsall, Manchester

OFFICE workers. Position your fax machine up
against your paper shredder. By aligning them
carefully together you can save hours of needless
paperwork by disposing of all incoming faxes the
moment they arrive.

> Paul Williams
> Kennington Oval, SE11

POWER station managers. Paint your chimneys white, with orange and yellow bases, to make it look like the ground is enjoying a cigarette. When the chimney is eventually demolished, ask the demolition men to paint it grey, beginning at the top and progressing downwards, occasionally 'flicking' off the tip using a demolition ball and chain, into a giant ashtray.

> John Gray
> Keighley

FOOTBALL managers. As teams invariably play better when 'reduced to ten men', why not start the match with only five players. This way, if your team plays crap you can change the whole lot of them, and still have your substitutes on the bench.

> Dave Lee
> Dorset

LIGHTHOUSE keepers. Amuse ships' captains by painting your lighthouse pink and the top purple, then standing on the top, getting the foghorn to go "Ugh! Ugh!" while you throw buckets of wallpaper paste up in the air.

> Ian Finlay
> Jedburgh

SATELLITE TV bosses. Save a fortune in broadcasting costs by switching off the Adult Channel at five past midnight. There's no point in broadcasting the remaining 3 hours and 55 minutes of porn. After five minutes all your viewers have already lost their mess, switched off and gone to bed.

> Mr Highbury
> Woolwich

ENJOY all the thrills and spills of professional
football management by driving to a motorway service
station with a friend and passing an envelope full of
Monopoly money backwards and forwards under the
table.

> Brian & Alex
> Thwaite

WORKERS hoping to have their "Workforce Request'
played on Virgin Radio should ensure that they list
only the singles which will be on the play list anyway.
Robert Palmer is your best bet.

> T.S.M.
> Littlehampton

FOOTBALL hooligans. Go to matches on horseback,
dressed as Mediaeval knights, and challenge the
mounted police officers to a jousting tournament.

> A. Armitage
> Penzance

PAUL Merson. At 60p a line Littlewood's Pools is a lot
cheaper than cocaine. And far less risky than the gee-
gees. Even a twat like you would have to be going some
to lose £300,000 at 60p a punt.

> S.A.
> London NW1

VICARS. When asked why almighty God permits so
much suffering in the world always couch your
answers in flowery, poetic prose which sounds wise
and meaningful but in actual fact means fuck all.
Phrases like "all part of a greater plan" and "the path
of life is many forked" always come in useful.

> Ann Atheist
> Whitley Bay

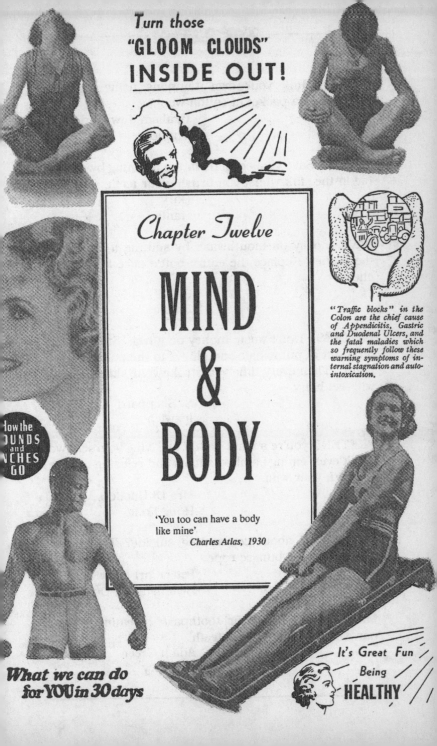

Turn those "GLOOM CLOUDS" INSIDE OUT!

Chapter Twelve

MIND & BODY

'You too can have a body like mine'
Charles Atlas, 1930

"*Traffic blocks*" in the Colon are the chief cause of Appendicitis, Gastric and Duodenal Ulcers, and the fatal maladies which so frequently follow these warning symptoms of internal stagnation and auto-intoxication.

How the POUNDS and INCHES GO

What we can do for YOU in 30 days

It's Great Fun Being HEALTHY

GIRLS. 'Roll your own' tampons using cigarette papers and a packet of cotton wool.

> Graham Townend
> Shipley

GENTS. Save vital seconds in the morning by urinating in the sink whilst you brush your teeth.

> Gary
> Hants.

SAVE money on mouthwash by spitting it back into the bottle. Replace the entire bottle once it becomes chewy.

> G. T.
> Shipley

BALDIES. Don't waste money on a rug. Simply snip off a tuft of pubic hair and glue it to the palm of your hand. Then every time you stroke your shiny head it will feel hairy.

> S. Sheppard
> Ipswich

PRETEND you're a giant panda by giving yourself two black eyes, eating bamboo shoots and refusing to have sex with your wife.

> Mrs Di Unetic
> Hong Kong

INDECISIVE about committing suicide? Then hang yourself with a bungee rope.

> Peter Carl Fenwick
> Beamish, Co. Durham

MAKE 'chocolate flavour' toothpaste by eating a Mars bar whilst brushing your teeth.

> Adam Creen
> Newbury

MAKE your neighbours think you're a doctor by leaving the house in the middle of the night carrying a small leather bag, then returning home half an hour later. Repeat this action up to six times every night.

P. C.
Leicester

LIVE every day as if it were your last by converting your bedroom into an intensive care ward, inserting pipes into your nose and arms, and lying in bed all day, saying and doing nothing.

Mrs T. Bolus
Spittle

MAKE people in the pub think you're a doctor by carrying a small leather bag and not laughing at the words 'penis', 'clitoris' or 'scrotum'.

P.C.
Leicester

ASK your barber to save your hair clippings. In later life these can be made into a wig, and will match your remaining hair perfectly.

> Yasmin Fletcher
> Priestley

DISCARDED cigarette butts make economical and efficient ear plugs, and also reduce the levels of nicotine entering your ears as a result of passive smoking.

> Simon Handley
> Edinburgh

MANCHESTER United fans. Avoid an asymmetrical muscular bulge on your right arm by masturbating alternately with your left hand.

> Gregory Clarke
> London NW4

MAKE the man in the off licence think you're a doctor by going in early every morning carrying your small leather bag and buying a large bottle of gin.

> P.C.
> Leicester

WEIGHT watchers. Avoid that devilish temptation to nibble at the chocolate bar in the cupboard or fridge by not buying the fucking thing in the first place, you fat bastards.

> Anthony Simcox
> France

DYSLEXICS. Try deliberately spelling words wrongly. This way at least you have a chance of spelling them correctly.

> Phil Wasley
> Liverpool

ATTEMPT your own corrective laser eye surgery by removing the back of your CD player and then staring into it whilst it is turned on.

> P.S.
> Leicester

BEARDED men can obtain the appearance of an upper class Arctic explorer by simply applying Tippex to their beards, painting their noses blue, and cutting off a couple of toes. It never fails to impress the girls.

> Ben Collins
> Galashiels

WELL-TO-DO middle and upper class people. Avoid feelings of guilt due to your privileged lifestyle by going to church regularly and prescribing to a doctrine based upon one or other interpretation of certain parts of the Bible. Simply re-interpret - or completely ignore - any parts of the Bible which are incompatible with your own lifestyle of greed and affluence.

> Mr S. Ford-Bridges
> London SW1

OVERWEIGHT, unemployed men. Get a well paid job in pantomime this winter by wearing a leotard and a long blonde wig. If you smile enough and flex your arms a bit, you'll be mistaken for a glamorous female 'Gladiator'.

J. Thwaite
Fulchester

BOOK 'Lipo-Suction' sessions as close to Christmas as possible. This way money can be saved by using your excess fat to baste the turkey and roast the potatoes.

A. L.
Ardley

HAVING problems removing your children's heads from iron railings? No need to call the Fire Brigade. Simply pop a lubricated condom on each of the child's ears, and gently pull them free.

Mr N. Roast
Aberness

GIVE up smoking by sticking one cigarette from each new pack up a fat friend's arse, filter first, then replacing it in the box. The possibility of putting that one in your mouth will put you off smoking any of them.

Harold Fletcher
Maiden Castle

WEEDY fellas. Develop a right arm like Arnold Schwarzenegger in a matter of weeks by investing in the latest Workout Video by Cindy Crawford.

B. Beater
St Annes

Fig. 3.—Diagram of
Flame's Head-dress

Chapter Thirteen

STYLE
&
PANACHE

'My clothes must be comfortable
to wear as well as look good'
Alvin Stardust, 1976

WHILST on holiday always wear a paper hat with the date and your holiday destination written clearly on the front. In years to come this will enable you to identify holiday snaps with ease.

> Ken Road
> Luton

MAN. UNITED fans. Don't waste money on yet another replica team strip. Simply strap a large plastic penis to your forehead. It will then be perfectly obvious to everybody which team you support.

> T. Worthington
> Altrincham

AT weddings make sure all the guests wear a paper hat with their names clearly written on the front. This will enable you to identify old faces from the past when viewing the pictures in years to come.

> Ken Road
> Luton

HAT wearers. Beat the wind by wearing a velcro head-band and stitching a strip of Velcro around the inside your hat .

> Brian C. Smith
> Edinburgh

LADIES. Knock 'em dead at Ascot this year by going into your garage or garden shed, getting the biggest thing you can find, and wearing it on your head.

> M. Samson
> Didburyshire

AT weddings ask the bride or groom to wear a sand-wich board with their names, the date, and the name of the church etc. written on it in bold letters.

> Ken Road
> Luton

MODERNISE old fashioned flared trousers by removing a triangle of cloth from the bottom of each leg and sewing the gap closed. The spare triangles can then be attached to a length of string and used as bunting to decorate your street on party occasions such as Royal anniversaries, weddings etc. Sombre bunting from black trousers could be used for the Queen Mother's funeral.

> J. Black
> Fulchester

DON'T throw away old socks with holes in the toe. Simply cut off the whole toe, turn the sock around and sew up the other end. Hey presto! A new sock.

> A. White
> Kettering

MODERNISE old fashioned 'drainpipe' trousers by making a slit in each leg and sewing in triangles of cloth removed from a length of bunting. Hey presto! Fashionable flares.

> J.Black
> Fulchester

CAN'T afford expensive tights? A pair of stockings stapled into a pair of underpants makes a cheap but effective alternative.

> P. Melba
> Onslow

SCOTCH perverts. Attach your kilt to your belt with curtain rings. You can then expose yourself quickly and effortlessly by simply drawing your kilt too and fro. A simple draw string mechanism, available from all curtain shops, can be added later if required.

> S. Cheesecake
> Rotherham

GIRLS. A saucy 'rubber fetish' style suspender belt can be made from an old bicycle inner tube and four elastic bands. Slip the tube around your waist with the four bands hanging from it, with a crocodile clip stuck to the bottom of each one.

C. Gateau
Hebden Bridge

REDUCE wear and tear on your work clothes by 20% by simply staying in bed on Mondays and not going to work.

T. Sponge
Dunbar

COAL MEN. Save having to wash your clothes by taking a night time job delivering sacks of flour.

J. R. Polley
Yeovil

CUT old dress trousers into 'slices' with garden shears. The resulting cloth rings make an excellent supply of spare hat bands.

Mrs J. Tapioca
Wivenhoe

ON TRAINS the plastic triangular packs in which sandwiches are sold make ideal elbow protectors. Wear them on your sleeves to prevent your elbows getting wet when your coffee gets spilled all over the table.

C. A. Mints
Fulham

DON'T throw away that old dart. Once removed the flight makes four excellent feathers for use in conjunction with spare hat bands.

Mrs J. Tapioca
Wivenhoe

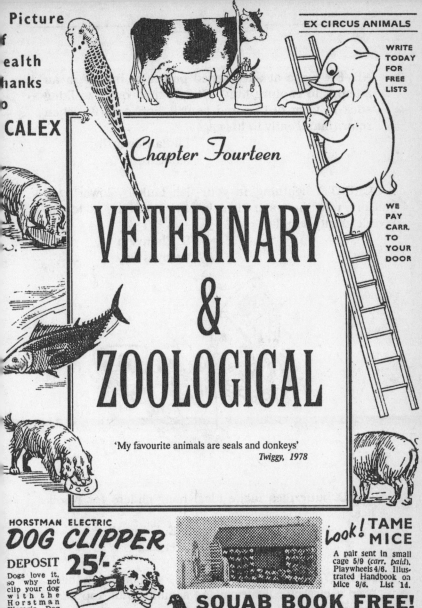

Picture
f
ealth
hanks
o

CALEX

Chapter Fourteen

VETERINARY
&
ZOOLOGICAL

'My favourite animals are seals and donkeys'
Twiggy, 1978

NEVER lunge at an escaped parrot or budgie in an attempt to capture him. Simply hold out a walking stick in front of him and he will 'hop' onto it. Then return him gently to his cage.

> Linda Howarth
> Manchester

CREATE 'lightning' in your fish tank by lowering a fork into the water then briefly connecting it to the electricity supply.

> S. Thomson
> Wemyss Bay

DEAD butterflies make ideal hang gliders for wood lice.

> A. E. Greenall
> Liverpool

MAGGOTS make ideal 'sausages' for mice. Cook them over a cigarette lighter using a milk bottle top as a mouse mini 'frying pan'.

> B. Newton
> Liverpool

A COCKTAIL stick, marble and a key ring make the perfect javelin, shot putt and hammer for your rodent decathlon.

A. E. Greenall
Liverpool 12

FIND out how many of your cat's lives are remaining by hitting it repeatedly with a mallet. The number of strokes required to bring about its demise will correspond with the number of lives that remained.

Mr G. Stone
Brighton

GRANDAD'S old army helmet, painted green and placed on a roller skate, makes an ideal playmate for lonely pet tortoises.

Phil W.
Liverpool

IT is easier to sharpen the end of a worm into a point using a pencil sharpener if you freeze it first.

K. Newton
Burnley

HALF a table tennis ball with an elastic band attached makes an ideal 'safety helmet' for your pet hamster, and significantly reduces the risk of head injury should he fall whilst using his exercise wheel.

> Mr C. Cream
> Bisley

TREAT your cat by placing a mouse in matchbox and feeding it on milk powder. Hey presto! 'Veal' mice.

> B. Labone
> Kirby

CIRCUMCISE your randy dog by attaching sandpaper 'chaps' to the bottom of your trouser legs.

> P.T.
> Garston

AN OLD spectacle lens makes an ideal and easily fitted 'sunroof' for a tortoise.

> J. Dodger
> Milton Keynes

PREPARE baby turtles for their hectic life at sea by placing them in a washing machine. Add salt instead of soap and you have the perfect 'ocean simulator'.
> S.P.
> Dundee

A SHEET of thick plywood cut into small cubes makes ideal 'Liquorice Allsorts' for sweet toothed woodpeckers or wood worms.
> K. Warton
> Stamford

EMPTY pot pourri bags make ideal 'sacks' for mouse sack races.
> A. E. Greenall
> Liverpool 12

FARMERS. Get butter out of your cows by 'rodeo riding' them for an hour or two before milking time.
> Volker Holz
> Fuerth, Germany

PLACE sprouts beneath a tortoise to increase its apparent number of legs.
> Kate Hunt
> Silverstone

PIG farmers. Paint toilet roll tubes black, then fill them with snow. Hey presto! Liquorice Allsorts for pigs, with no sugar to harm their teeth.
> K. Wharton
> Stamford

HALF a horse chestnut conker shell would make a frightening hat for a tortoise.
> P. Beetroot
> Cubbard

FARMERS. Minor skin grafts can be performed on pigs by covering any cuts and grazes with thin strips of bacon.

> Phil Wasey
> Liverpool

A SIMPLE drinking straw, cut into small lengths, will make sufficient batons for up to six rodent display teams. Alternately, one straw makes a first class 'pole' for rodent pole vaulters.

> T. Silver
> Newbury

CARDBOARD hats worn by McDonalds staff make ideal canoes for guinea pigs. And the plastic tea stirrers are perfect oars.

> A. E. Greenall
> Liverpool 12

WINKLE shells make ideal turbans for field mice requiring an exotic look.

> John Tait
> Thropton

RACE 'homing goldfish' by flushing them all down the lavatory. Leave all your taps running and see which one returns first.

> J. King
> Oswestry

WATER filled fire extinguishers make ideal 'oxygen cylinders' for dolphins should they be taken out of the water at any time, for transportation etc.

> P. Field
> Sussex

Chapter Fifteen

FUN
&
GAMES

'P.L.A.Y., play playaway, away play a playaway play away, a play away Playaway'
Briant Cant, 1973

'Did he really make that piano himself?' a girl whispered.

CONVINCE dinner guests that your wife has a tape-worm by teaching her to regurgitate noodles while you hold a spoonful of sugar to her mouth.

> Mr D. Light-Infantry
> Gateshead

DON'T waste your money on Christmas singles this year. Come December just listen to normal singles, and shake some sleigh bells towards the end of the record.

> F. Park
> Portsmouth

PRETEND you've reached the 'Eliminator' stage on Gladiators by running the wrong way up an escalator in Marks and Spencers.

> P.W.
> Merseyside

A SIMPLE pocket calculator placed alongside your television is a constant source of amusement. Watch your friends' faces as they try in vain to change the TV channel with it.

> P.T.
> Aigburth

THIS summer make snow for the kids by grating ice from your freezer compartment with a cheese grater.

> Mrs R. Tea
> Stafford

WIMBLEDON tennis organisers. Why not play the finals on the first day of the championships, instead of the last. That way the grass will all be green, and the players will have a decent surface on which to display their undoubted talents.

> Laurie Penfold
> Sheffield

AVOID the dangers of cycling on Britain's overcrowded roads by simply making a video of your next car journey, and then watching it whilst peddling away on an exercise bike in front of your television.

Pete T.
Liverpool

LEARNER skateboarders. Carry an old paint roller in each hand. These can be used as 'stabilisers' whenever you lose your balance.

Desmond Umbridge
Bolton

CONVINCE the birds you're a top professional footballer by calling them a taxi, then pulling the door off when it arrives, and kicking shit out of the driver.

Mr C. Bell
Manchester

POKER players. An old scrubbing brush upturned on the table is ideal for standing your cards upright in, leaving both hands free to pour whisky, light cigarettes, adjust your hat, etc.

B. C. Smith
Edinburgh

MAKE a kaleidoscope for kids by stretching cling film over the end of a toilet roll tube and dropping a few pieces of broken coloured glass inside. Remember to tell your kids to always point it downwards when looking in the open end.

Mr A. Gemmill
Nottingham

HOLD an impromptu reunion of all your relatives, most of whom you haven't seen for years, by simply winning the lottery. Hey presto! Just watch the free-loading fuckers turn up by the car load, all wanting a slice of the action.

Leighton Calvert
Edinburgh

SAVE all the time and effort involved in playing fruit machines by simply sending all your money to the fruit machine manufacturers together with a note asking them to send 70% of it back to you.

> G. Hawkins
> Brighton

PLAY 'McDonalds Drive Thru' with your kiddies by getting them to ride past the living room window on their tricycles and order what they want for tea. Then let them ride to the kitchen window where you hand them something completely different to eat. Unless they ordered fish fingers, in which case you tell them to park on the flower bed and wait for half an hour until they're ready.

> J. McGovern
> Nottingham

FETE organisers. Put a copy of the Readers Digest on your tombola stall. Then write to them saying that THEY have been entered in YOUR prize draw.

> T. Snaith
> Blyth

KIDS. Hide single serving tomato sauce sachets under your Action Man's clothing to add extra realism when he is bayonetted or stabbed during play battles.

> Y. Gray
> Evesham

BUDDING tennis stars. Practice playing in front of your bedroom mirror using an old electric guitar as a substitute racket.

> J. Clark
> Huddersfield

Chapter Sixteen

CHEESE
&
ONION

'They think its all over... It is now.'
Kenneth Wolstenholme, 1966

**The 15 members of
the Bedding Guild**

STEAL money from flat-mates by borrowing £5 then moving to Fife. (If you live in Fife, move to South Fife.)

Anon.
Fife

ALWAYS allow bald people to go in front of you in lavatory queues, as the loss of hair and onset of incontinence are usually simultaneous in middle aged men.

A. Adderstone
Bemerside

GIVE off-duty policemen a taste of their own medicine by stopping them in the street and asking them where they're going.

C. Arrow
Norwich

A STRIP of black cardboard about two inches wide, worn over the eyes, makes a perfect disguise for Lottery or Pools winners wishing to conceal their identity.

Mark Anderson
West Hampstead

PRACTICE being a paramedic by standing on the top deck of a bus, holding old ladies hands and telling them "everything's going to be alright".

J. Edwards
Staffordshire

EXPERIENCE the luxury of staying in a top hotel by keeping your fridge in the bedroom, filling it with chocolate, peanuts and drinks, and then burning a twenty pound note every time you eat or drink anything.

S. Park
Wimbledon

FED UP with fast food restaurants? Empty a tin of vegetable soup on their doorstep. It'll look like one of their customers has thrown up.

Scott Shaw
Hemel Hempstead

FELLAS. Keep a pile of bricks together with the names and addresses of all your ex girlfriends next to the telly so that if your lottery numbers come up you can go straight round their houses and put their windows out. It will serve them right for dishing the dirt on you in the papers later that week, which they're bound to do.

B. Labone
Everton

CREATE the atmosphere of a top Soho sex club in your own home by getting your wife to remove her top and bring you a bottle of cheap champagne, then return ten minutes later with a bill for £500.

S. Park
Wimbledon

OLD LADIES. Worried some poor sod who's late for his bus is going to get past you on the pavement? Simply wander aimlessly from from left to right. That will stop them.

Mark Giddings
Bristol

BLINK alternately with one eye, and then the other, whilst watching TV soaps. This way you'll never miss a second. If you add it all up you probably miss up to an hour of your favourite programmes each year due to normal blinking.

J. Pears
Wimbledon

AVOID being murdered, raped, held hostage in a siege, poisoned, stabbed to death and buried under a patio, blown up by religious extremists, falling victim to a fatal mystery virus, embroiled in a drug war, burgled, falsely imprisoned, blackmailed and probably murdered again by simply not moving to one of the seven houses in Brookside Close.

P. Redmond
Liverpool

RE-CREATE the effect of watching satellite television by going to a multi-screen movie complex and walking to and fro between cinemas watching two minutes of each film at a time, but not really paying attention to any of them. Then, at midnight, nip into a nearby adult cinema to watch ten minutes of a third rate porn movie before going home to bed.

P. Croft
Blyth

INDIE bands. When you finally get to appear on 'Top Of The Pops' after years and years of playing the gig circuit, sending demos to John Peel and traipsing around every record company in London, don't forget to stand there looking miserable, as if its the last place in the world you want to be.

C. Sanders
Kentucky

SIAMESE twins. A padded 'Ultrabra' makes a handy pair of skateboarding safety helmets.

B. McMahon
Edinburgh

The End